PRAYERS
FOR
LAY MINISTRY

Carl T. Uehling

FORTRESS PRESS

Philadelphia

*Library of Congress Catalog Card Number
73-88341*

ISBN 0-8006-1062-8

4051H73   Printed in U.S.A.   1-1062

For my parents

CONTENTS

II. PRAYERS FOR
LAY MINISTRY IN THE CHURCH

III. PRAYERS FOR
LAY MINISTRY AMONG FRIENDS
AND FAMILY

PREFACE

LIFE TENDS to be punctuated by prayer, even when those who are doing the praying are not especially religious! Because of custom and heritage we nod to God periodically, often as a way of beginning and ending things, and thus is formed a kind of continuing liturgy whether we approve of it or not.

Certainly someone needs to wonder if the reading of a prayer at the start of the weekly Kiwanis meeting constitutes a religious activity. Such praying is admittedly perfunctory, contrived, often even hypocritical. If the best of prayers are those that reveal a genuine sense of communion between a believer and his Lord, the kind that fit into an agenda are probably the worst.

But they are better, still, than none at all, and that's the point. Our communication with one another frames our relationships, and the dutiful husband kisses his wife goodbye in the morning without much thought, but the absence of that kiss would suggest something about the quality of the marriage. We say hello and ask about the state of the other's health, and if our sincerity might be questioned it could at least be claimed that the proprieties are in some vague sense just that: proper.

Many of the prayers in this volume are proper in that same vague sense. They presume

no supreme spiritual insights, but simply a time when someone should say, "Let us pray."
They are intended as a help and a guide for those who find themselves called upon to pray in public. They are far from the heights of the communication possible between a believer and his God, but they are, at the least, an acknowledgement that, yes, there is a someone to whom we are addressing ourselves.

But these prayers are also intended to be heard by others, with some exceptions. Not overheard by them, but rather perceived in the sense that the one doing the praying is speaking on behalf of those others as well. Since these prayers ought to meet the needs of both the one doing the praying and those others who are listening in, they constitute a tool for ministry.

A minister is generally understood to be a person ordained by a church. But ministry is what happens when Christians reach with God's love into the heart of life. Thus all Christians are ministers, and they minister by their concern for others, concern which they show by their deeds of active service in the face of human need.

One way to minister is to pray with others. It isn't the only way, of course, and certainly never an all-sufficient way. But praying, at the start of a meeting or at the hospital bed of a sick friend or with the children at bedtime, is a form of ministry.

This book is for lay ministry. It offers over a hundred simple prayers designed for dozens of ordinary and extraordinary circumstances in life when laypeople might be called on to pray. It doesn't cover every possible circumstance. Hopefully the ministry of the believer will uncover other opportunities for prayer. These prayers will at least show that public prayer need not be elaborate and may serve as models for other prayers of the believer's own composition.

These are Christian prayers. They do not offend the beliefs of others, but they are in the name of Christ. That might be a problem in some places and at some times, but praying, at the very least, is surely an act of faith, on the part of the one doing the praying. We must minister with love and consideration for all people, but as those who believe that Jesus Christ is their Lord.

CARL T. UEHLING

September 22, 1973
Philadelphia, Pa.

I. PRAYERS FOR

LAY MINISTRY IN THE WORLD

The prayers in this section try to anticipate the various occasions when a person may be asked to pray within the life of the community. Even though society is becoming increasingly secular, it is reluctant to ignore the custom of acknowledging the existence and benevolence of a deity, and to whatever degree we believe that a people ought to have some understanding of its relationship to God, to that degree we will see the sense of the continuance of the custom.

When you pray, as circumstance gives opportunity, do so with conviction and clarity, believing that it is a way of ministering to others, not that they might miraculously be converted or led into the church, but that the needs of the immediate occasion might be met. That need could be nothing more complicated than a harmonious business meeting, but in asking God's help to such an end, you will have ministered in the name of Christ.

A MEETING OF A CIVIC CLUB
OR ASSOCIATION

FATHER, you know that we have very little in
common. Our vocations cover the wide range of
our community's needs, and our politics present
opposing points of view, and even our faith in
you is subject to a variety of interpretations.

For all of our differences, however, we are
alike in our humanity and in our need for your
love. Remind us of all we hold in common.
Yet grant us also the ability to affirm our
distinctions without hurt, one to another.

So may our gathering be to our mutual
service and to the service of our fellowman;
through Jesus Christ, our Lord. Amen.

FATHER, we acknowledge you as the creator
of all that exists, and we look to you for
direction as we confront the various issues of
life. We are grateful for that direction as it
has helped to mold the history of our nation,
and as it has had its influence within the
circumstances of our personal affairs.

Continue to be concerned for us, we pray.
Be with our organization, and give us the
desire to reach beyond ourselves in order to

meet the needs of your people. Move within the leaders of our community, that they might govern wisely and honestly for the common good. Be our chief guest at this meeting, and strengthen us by our nourishment and fellowship; through Christ, our Lord. Amen.

ETERNAL GOD, we know that you are the author and creator of our world, and that because of your design we have enough for all our needs. We thank you for our pleasant earth and for all that we understand by our own experience in life to be from your love.

Be with us at this time as we gather together. Help us to know one another better, especially if we have conflicting opinions on the issues of the day. Give us a new resolve to work for the improvement of our community, and help us to control whatever might hinder our ability to meet in unity and mutual respect.

Grant that this time might be one of accomplishment and concord; through Christ, our Lord. Amen.

A CITY COUNCIL MEETING

LORD, we live in a land where we have the
freedom to take part in the process by which
we are governed. Those who are about to meet
have been chosen to represent us and our points
of view. They face the temptation to forget us,
or ignore us, or go contrary to our needs. Save
them from this possibility, and work within
them that they might be reminded of their
duty to the people. Because you are a God of
righteousness and truth and justice, let those
virtues prevail within this body; through
Christ, our Lord. Amen.

A SCHOOL BOARD MEETING

FATHER, our community has given us a
special responsibility to be concerned about
the education of our children. They are a trust
from your love, and we are grateful for them.

Guide us now, that we may perceive their
educational needs and seek to meet those needs
regardless of personalities or politics. They have
no defense against our failures. For their sake
help us to succeed; through Christ, our Lord.
Amen.

A PATRIOTIC OCCASION

ETERNAL GOD, our Father, your law has prevailed across the years, and you are the source of justice and truth. We acknowledge you as our Lord, and commend our nation to your guidance and protection.

Instill within our people a determination to participate in the affairs of government, and give us good judgment as we select our leaders. Save us from the conceit of believing that you favor our land over any others, but turn us to the meeting of the needs of people at home and abroad.

Let our nation, Father, stand for compassion and service and, above all else, for peace; through Christ, our Lord. Amen.

A POLITICAL MEETING

LORD GOD, come with your Spirit to this meeting, for if ever we need your influence, it is when we participate in the process by which we are governed.

We will be tempted in the time ahead to judge others falsely, to love ourselves, and to believe that the ends we seek can justify any means we employ. Help us rise above such mischief.

Nor let us indulge ourselves with self-righteousness, as if we possessed all virtue and our opposition were all evil. Remind us that the truth depends upon the dialogue of differing opinions and is best achieved when a free and open forum is provided.

To that end, O Lord, come to this place and this assembly, that we might by our efforts increase the freedom of our people and their determination to seek truth and justice and peace; through Christ, our Lord. Amen.

A CORPORATION'S
BOARD OF DIRECTORS' MEETING

ETERNAL GOD, our lives and our times are in
your hands, and our accomplishments are as
nothing in your sight. Yet you have given us
this earth and its resources for our use, and as
we are able to serve your people by our
endeavors, we fulfill your design and purpose.

Keep us more concerned for the doing of
your will than for the gaining of reward. Guide
us as we set our priorities so that we will
meet the needs of those to whom we have
responsibilities. Remind us that even in the
world of business with its competition and
intrigue and selfishness we work best as we
work by your precepts, and help us resist the
temptation to ignore your will for the sake of
personal advantage.

Give us a sense of your presence during
this meeting and a determination to serve you
in the ordering of our affairs; through Christ,
our Lord. Amen.

A CUB SCOUT MEETING

GREAT SPIRIT, we want to do our duty to you
by our lives of loving service to other people.
Direct us so that we can be fair to everybody,
follow those who are our leaders, and help our
pack to go and grow. Show us how to smile at
our friends and how to help them in their lives.
Teach us your truth; through Christ, our Lord.
Amen.

A BOY SCOUT MEETING

GOD, OUR FATHER, we trust in you and
believe that you have created us and all that
exists. Be with us now during this meeting
of our troop. Help us to be considerate of
each other and to learn not only the lore of
scouting but also new ways of helpfulness
and service; through Christ, our Lord. Amen.

A GIRL SCOUT MEETING

O LORD, our God, give your direction to our
meeting, and help what we do here to be of
service to others. Show us how we can be
friends with those we meet and sisters to other
scouts. Keep us clean in thought, word, and
deed, and willing to do our duty to you and
our country; through Christ, our Lord. Amen.

BEFORE A LITTLE LEAGUE GAME

FATHER, help us play good ball in this game, to work together as a team and not for our individual glory. Help us play to win, but because we cannot always win, help us to lose well if we must lose.

Give us respect for the other team, and if it should seem as if we are being badly used, keep our heads cool and our mouths quiet. Let this be a good game, Father, for both sides; in the name of Jesus. Amen.

AN OCCASION HONORING ATHLETES

WE ARE TOGETHER this evening, Father,
because through this past year people from
this school competed in various kinds of sports.
We are here to recognize and honor them.

Remind us, however, that we cannot always
win, and that someone must always lose,
and that it is far better to know how to lose
than it is to be able to win.

Now grace this time with your presence.
Help us to realize that all we have, food and
clothing, friends and family, winning and
losing, comes from you; in Jesus' name. Amen.

ON THE GIVING OF ATHLETIC AWARDS

FATHER, we've worked hard this year, all of
us, teachers and staff and students, coaches and
managers and players. Sometimes we've
succeeded, and sometimes we've failed.
Sometimes we've won, and sometimes we've
lost. Through it all we've trusted in your
presence, and now at the end of the year, at this
time for thinking about where we've been and
what we've done, we ask you to be with us too.

Keep us humble, and honest, and willing to
acknowledge that all we are and have comes
from you. So may we seek to serve you by the
way we live; through Christ, our Lord. Amen.

A RETIREMENT DINNER
FOR A CO-WORKER

FATHER, we are here to honor a good friend
who is coming to the end of his(her) work with us.
Through the years we have valued him(her) highly
for his(her) craftsmanship, his(her) understanding,
his(her) wisdom. In the day-by-day conduct of our
affairs he(she) has been kind and considerate, and
we know that we will be diminished because
he(she) is no longer with us. We thank you for
his(her) contribution and rejoice in the life and
work which we have shared.

Now we take joy in the coming of a new
stage of life for our friend. Grant that he(she) may
have contentment, but fill his(her) days with
challenge as well. You know as we do his(her)
worth in your world. Use him(her) in the future as
in the past to accomplish your will. Give him(her)
many happy hours, and the assurance of your
love.

Now be with us as we gather around this
table and share this meal. Strengthen us,
Father, that we may serve you and one another;
through Christ, our Lord. Amen.

AN ELEMENTARY SCHOOL GRADUATION

FATHER, we are here to celebrate the accomplishment of these young people who have successfully completed a stage in their education. We thank you for the help they have received from you, especially as you have reached to them through their teachers, advisors, and parents.

We thank you for the opportunity of education itself, so that people can learn about your world, and prepare themselves to participate usefully and happily in its life.

We ask you to continue to work with these graduates as they enter a new school. Give them confidence to cope with the unfamiliar and the strange, and willingness to work to the extent of their ability. Keep them aware of your interest in them and their affairs. Even as they meet new friends and encounter new ideas help them to mature with an understanding of your truth and a determination to live in your way; through Jesus Christ, our Lord. Amen.

A HIGH SCHOOL GRADUATION

FATHER, in this country more than eight million people are graduating from high school this year, some of them from this institution today. We are here because we are their friends and their families, and we care about them.

We know you care about them too. They are among millions, yet you know each one by name. Your love for them, each one, is deeper than that of a parent or a mate.

Nor is there even any need for us to ask you to continue to care for them. The record of your love is clear across the years.

We pray, therefore, not for your presence but for our awareness of it; not for your continuing guidance in the lives of those we honor today, but for their continuing faith in you. It is so big a world, and they are so few among eight million. But it is your world, and they are your children.

We commend them to you, now in this exalted moment of their lives, even as we know you will never leave them through all that lies ahead; in the name of Jesus. Amen.

A VOCATIONAL SCHOOL GRADUATION

DEAR FATHER, the days of preparation have come to their end, and these young people are ready to take their places in your world with their talents and skills.

We are thankful for the training they have received, and for those who have been their teachers. We ask for your help in their future, that they might continue to improve their abilities and discover rich satisfactions in their work.

Enable them to see what they do as a means of serving your people, even as they have been served by this school. We pray this in the name of one who was once a carpenter, even Jesus Christ, your Son, our Lord. Amen.

A COLLEGE GRADUATION

O LORD GOD, Father of us all, we celebrate today the achievement of those who graduate from this institution, and pray for your presence with them at this time and in the time to come.

They are a measure of our hope for our world and its future. We place much trust in their skills, their understandings, their willingness to serve.

Yet we know that as we have often failed, they will fail; as we have often acted unwisely, they will also ignore their better judgment; as we have sometimes been cruel and arrogant and selfish, they will be human too.

For their future and for our future we can best hope in you. Uphold us when we fail. Instruct us when our wisdom is not enough for our circumstance. Reprove us when we seek our own good at the expense of others, and continue to teach us your ways of love and peace; through Christ, our Lord. Amen.

FOR PEOPLE ON WELFARE

LORD JESUS CHRIST, you were dependent upon the generosity of friends through the years of your ministry, and you clearly taught that as we help others in their need, we do so as unto you.

Give us a better understanding of your people who are forced to live on welfare. We tend to see them as those who will not work for their living, yet most are rather those who are unable by infirmity or circumstance to support themselves. Make us more tolerant of their condition, and direct us to work for a society in which the needs of people will be met without humiliation and with justice. Amen.

FOR CHRISTIANS AND JEWS

FOR TOO LONG, Father, bitter hatred has continued between those who name the name of Christ and the Jewish people. Yet we know how wrong that has been and that our faith cannot permit us to hate anyone, especially the Jews, for Christ himself was a Jew.

Help us to translate our faith into works, dear God, to speak out when prejudice is expressed, to act when others are being oppressed because of their heritage or beliefs. Beyond that give us opportunities to learn about our brothers the Jews, to work with them to our community's good, and to heal the wounds of the past; through Christ, our Lord. Amen.

FOR A TIME OF RACIAL TENSION

ETERNAL GOD, we believe that all men are
created equal, and that our human efforts to
divide and isolate and oppress because of racial
divisions are contrary to your will. We have tried
to overcome those divisions but we have failed.

Now people are hating one another without
knowing one another, solely on the basis of their
color. Turn us away from such stupidity. Bring
us to our senses, and open our eyes to the
possibilities that continue to exist for your
people to live together and work together
without thought for the differences between
them by reason of their race. Save us from
arrogance and condescension and strife, and
lead us to new levels of unity and peace;
through Christ, our Lord. Amen.

FOR A CHANGING NEIGHBORHOOD

FATHER, we are grateful for our homes and our
neighbors, but there are those who are concerned
because they are afraid of change.

Help us to realize that all people are your
people. Give us patience and a willingness to
learn when we think we are threatened.
Encourage us to see our calling as believers in
you, so that we will look for ways to increase
understanding and good will among all people;
in the name of Jesus Christ. Amen.

FOR THE WISE USE OF THE EARTH

DEAR GOD, we praise you for our earthly home designed according to your perfect plan and able to meet the needs of all your people. We praise you for the beauty of nature, for the marvel of life, for the richness that surrounds us.

Yet, O Lord, we know that we are exhausting the resources of this world and endangering our lives and the lives of our descendents by our reckless use of what you have given.

Bring us to our senses, and remind us that these magnificent treasures will vanish if we do not exercise restraint. Turn us around before it is too late, and help us see that greater joy which can come from conserving instead of expending; through Christ, our Lord. Amen.

FOR ECOLOGY

TEACH US HOW to use the earth wisely, Father. In our haste to surround ourselves with modern marvels we have polluted our air and water and robbed the soil of its nutrients; to gain mineral wealth we have destroyed vast land areas.

Show us how to conserve what you have given us, to be content with a simpler but cleaner world, to find greater values in your natural design than in our mechanized improvements; through Christ, our Lord. Amen.

FOR A TIME OF FAMINE OR DISASTER

BEHOLD YOUR PEOPLE, O God, and visit
them in their great need with your love. Open
the hearts of those who are blessed with plenty
that they will share of their abundance, and
move any who have helping skills to volunteer
their time and talent.

Guide your people through this season of
adversity, and give them new determination
to work together for the common good;
through Christ, our Lord. Amen.

FOR DAILY WORK

ETERNAL GOD, we thank you for our work in
life, for the skills we have received and the
opportunities that have opened to us to
contribute to society's good and support
ourselves and our loved ones.

Help us to be diligent and honest in our
labors. Turn us away from the temptation to
slothfulness or apathy and keep us alert to the
ways in which we can serve others by what we do.

Increase our courage if inadequate working
conditions require our action for a righting of
the wrongs, yet show us how to be supportive
of competent and judicious management.

Your Son was a carpenter, Father. Direct us
that we might see our work as a fulfillment of
his will. In his name we pray. Amen.

FOR FARMERS

FATHER, we pray for those who till the soil, whose labor gains from the earth the very sustenance of our lives.

You know how much they are dependent upon factors beyond their control, such as the weather and the conditions of their markets. You know, as well, the rigors of their work, the long hours they must spend in the fields, the uncertainty that haunts their endeavors.

Give them patience in adversity and an understanding of the importance of their role in our world. So may they know themselves to be your servants in their care of the earth, and find meaning for their lives in the necessities they supply for so many other lives; through Christ, our Lord. Amen.

FOR GOVERNMENTAL LEADERS

ETERNAL LORD, you are the ruler of nations, by your precepts our affairs are judged.

Look to those whom we have selected as our leaders. Impress upon them the importance of their responsibilities, but humble them by reminding them of their humanity and their weakness.

Hold before them the ideal of the greatest good for the greatest number, but make them aware, as well, of the rights of the smallest minority in our midst. Turn them away from intemperate decisions and aggressive actions, and into the paths of service for all the people; through Christ, our Lord. Amen.

FOR PEACE

FATHER GOD, for too long your people have used war as the ultimate means of resolving their differences, and millions have suffered greatly in every age because of our stupidity.

Teach us to seek peace and pursue it. Help us to select leaders who will govern wisely and well, and without resort to violence. Turn us away from the jealousy, prejudice, and hatred that make people ready to bear arms against others. Show us how to give a soft answer, and turn the other cheek, and love our enemies, as did the prince of peace, your Son, Jesus Christ, in whose name we pray. Amen.

II. PRAYERS FOR

LAY MINISTRY IN THE CHURCH

*Church people tend to think of their pastor
as the only minister in the congregation, and for
generations clergy have routinely been called
upon to pray as if they alone can be heard by
God. But this is beginning to change.*

*The average congregation's organized life,
for one thing, has proliferated to such an extent
that it is impossible for the pastor to be present
at every meeting. If there is to be a prayer at
all, someone else must do the praying.*

*But more importantly, we are coming to see
ordination apart from the more primitive
concepts that held holy men to be alone
qualified to enter the presence of God. Ministers
now serve best as they are able to help others
within their congregations to see their own roles
as ministers. Ministry is not what a single
"set-apart" person does, but what properly ought
to be the concern of all who believe.*

*These prayers anticipate the various possible
needs within a congregation's life. Some
adaptation may be necessary to fit the
circumstance, and probably every congregation
will have other occasions for which nothing
contained herein will be suitable. Perhaps, in
such cases, these prayers may prove to be
models for further compositions.*

A CONGREGATIONAL MEETING

DEAR FATHER, we are your people and we seek to live and govern ourselves in accordance with your will.

Now we are met in order to manage the affairs of our congregation, to hear reports, adopt a budget, and plan for the future. Send your Spirit, that what we do here may be more than the business of a corporation. Challenge us to concern ourselves for others rather than for ourselves, to see the building of your kingdom as our primary task, to reach beyond our own needs to the needs of your world.

Help us to differ honestly and in charity, and cause what we do to be a sign of your love for your world and your people; through Christ, our Lord. Amen.

COME, HOLY SPIRIT, to this assembly of believers. Fill us with love for one another and faith in you. Increase our determination to work for the building up of your church. Help us see the reports and statistics of this meeting as lively service to your people. Prevent us from being satisfied with ourselves and our accomplishments, but keep us as will from discouragement.

We believe this is your church, and that you will do your giid and gracious will among us. Come, O Spirit, and abide with us. Amen.

LORD JESUS CHRIST, you gave assurance that where two or three are gathered together in your name, you would also be present. Behold your people assembled in this place as those who follow your leadership and desire to build your kingdom.

Look upon this congregation, and see the difficulties we face and the problems that have no easy solution. Work through us now, that we might find answers to our needs.

Help us, as well, to draw closer one to another because of our faith in you, that we might live in love and mutual service, so that the world may see us and know by our lives that we believe in you. Amen.

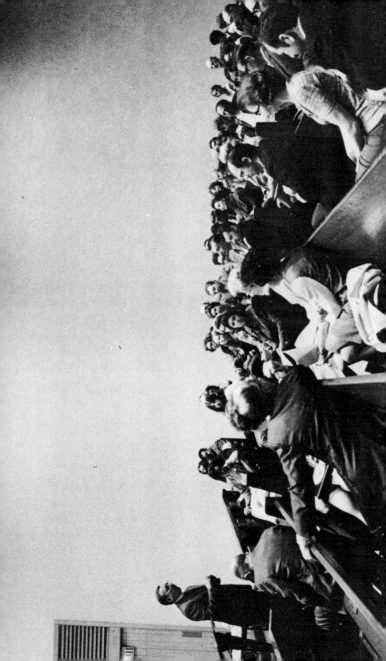

A CHURCH COUNCIL MEETING

WE ARE THANKFUL, Lord, for the trust the people of our congregation have placed in us by electing us to serve as members of the council.

But we are also very much aware of our limitations. We are not wise enough or patient enough or kind enough to serve well. We need your Spirit. Come and move through us, and cause what we do and say to be appropriate to the needs and a reflection of our faith in you and in your Son, Jesus Christ, in whose name we pray. Amen.

YOU KNOW WHAT we are like, Father, and you realize that some of us are here grudgingly, torn away from television or household chores; others of us are here pridefully, as if our position on this body made us better than others; and some of us are here with hidden agendas, intending to accomplish our own will for our own benefit.

Yet you take us as we are, despite our poor motivations, and you make use of us for the building of your kingdom. For this grace we give you our praise, and now, we pray, overcome our weaknesses with your strength, and cause your will to be done here on earth and in this church, as it is in heaven; through Christ, our Lord. Amen.

LORD JESUS CHRIST, you insisted that your disciples be concerned first of all for the things of your kingdom. Too often we worry about nonessentials and argue over trifles. Too easily we reduce our mission to the reporting of statistics or the balancing of budgets. Challenge us to see the greatest needs for your love, and overcome whatever reluctance we might have that could hinder us in our ministry, and help us to work together at this time and in the future so that our efforts might be a part of the building of your kingdom. Amen.

A WORSHIP AND MUSIC
COMMITTEE MEETING

FATHER GOD, we thank you for the heritage
of our faith, for all that is of value from the past.
We thank you, as well, for the challenge of the
present day and the promise of the future.

Much that is different is difficult for us to
understand, and often we resist change only
because of our fear or our pride. Send your
Spirit so that we may have the wisdom to
distinguish that which will be helpful to your
people and that which will only serve to divide
and obscure.

Enable us, as well, to have tolerance for
the feelings of others, and thus may we plan
services of worship that will glorify you and help
your people; through Christ, our Lord. Amen.

A CHRISTIAN EDUCATION
COMMITTEE MEETING

O LORD, we come here because of the responsibility we share for the education of your people. Especially do we desire to know about you and your will, so that in this congregation and within our community we might show the consequences of our faith in daily life.

Spark our imaginations and prod our creativity. Make us dissatisfied with ineffective methods and stifling routines. Give us a sense of the excitement that encourages a climate of learning, and work within us to preserve all that is good within our program even as we seek to bring new life where we are asleep or dead; in the name of Jesus. Amen.

A PROPERTY COMMITTEE MEETING

FATHER, we know that you are not
more present in temples we build than in the
other places of life. Yet your people need
special places that they can associate with your
service, and those places must be given care.

Help us to strike a proper balance between
the service of the place we call a church and the
service of your people who are the church.
By such perspective may we serve well in this
time, doing what must be done but for that
good which is greater than the care of things;
in the name of Jesus. Amen.

A FINANCE COMMITTEE MEETING

WE ARE ABOUT to spend much time discussing budgets and receipts and expenditures, Father, and you know the risk we run of forgetting that people and programs are behind the figures. Give us your grace, so that when we wonder where we will get the funds we need, we will remember that you are the source of all our treasure.

Give us, as well, a sense of priorities, lest our prudence interfere with the work of your kingdom or our extravagance deny to some because of its favor of others.

And grant us to see that it is only money with which we concern ourselves, a means of serving flesh and blood and not a value of itself, lest at the last we be found caring only for that which moths may consume or thieves break in and steal; through Christ, our Lord. Amen.

A YOUTH COMMITTEE MEETING

FATHER, our special concerns are the young people of our congregation and our community. We love them and deeply desire that they reach maturity well-equipped to live in service to your kingdom and to the world.

Yet we are tempted to mold them into our own image. Prevent us from that ambition, and give us the good sense to know the difference between imposing ourselves upon them and giving them the guidance they ought to have from us. By your Spirit direct what we do here, so that our young people may continue to find meaning and help within your church; through Christ, our Lord. Amen.

A SOCIAL MINISTRY COMMITTEE MEETING

LORD JESUS CHRIST, you made it clear that
if we gave a cup of cold water, or visited a
prisoner in a jail, it would be as if we were
serving you. All manner of human need, of all
dimensions, is properly our concern because
of your love for all of your people.

Now, we pray, point out to us the areas of
greatest need that can be touched by our
efforts. Do not let us become discouraged
because of those who might ridicule us or
oppose us through prejudice or ignorance.
Rather cause us to reach in concern even to
those who would cut short your kingdom's
work, and convert us to such a new understanding
of your will that we may build a world withour war,
poverty, disease, or oppression. Amen.

A WOMEN'S MEETING

O GOD, we look to you as our leader and guide, and trust in you to uphold and protect us through life. We thank you for every evidence we have of your love.

Now be with us as we meet together. Help us to learn more about your people and their work for your kingdom in other places.

Open us to the possibilities for innovation and real accomplishment. Prevent us from hindering your purposes because of our petty jealousies or hurt feelings. Give us a sense of unity and goodwill one to another, that what we do now may truly be in the name of your Son, Jesus Christ, our Lord. Amen.

HELP US, O God, lest in our concern for the business that is before us we forget our calling as Christians and our responsibility to love and serve each other. Keep clear before us the purposes of your kingdom, so that we can see the good that might be accomplished by our actions.

Inspire us as we consider your word and as we learn about your people, so that we can go from here more fully dedicated to you in our daily lives.

Be with those of our members who are absent, especially any who are ill or in affliction, and give us a full measure of your Spirit; through Christ, our Lord. Amen.

SPIRIT OF GOD, move in and through us even now, that the routine of our meeting may be filled with your presence, and transform our business according to your lively and exciting purposes.

Open us to the needs of your people in every place, and enable us to see what we can do for the poor, the oppressed, the sick, and the discouraged. Help us, as well, to reach to one another in loving concern, to touch our hurts with healing peace, to understand and care.

Save us from false pride and love of ourselves. Turn us away from waste and emptiness, and set us to the doing of those tasks that will build your kingdom; through Christ, our Lord. Amen.

A MEN'S MEETING

ETERNAL FATHER, you have called us apart from the world so that we might meet together in brotherhood, and we thank you for this opportunity.

Hold before us the example of your Son, who was the man who lived for others, and show us the ways in which we can reach to human need. To that end let our meeting have its purpose.

Then grant us grace that in going forth from here we may witness to your truth by our lives, and keep us faithful to our calling as those who name Jesus Christ as Lord, through whom we pray. Amen.

O SPIRIT OF GOD, you call us to faith in Jesus Christ as our Lord; you gather us into his church on earth that we might serve him; and we believe that you have brought us to this time together for the purposes of the kingdom.

Help us to see clearly those purposes, lest in our preoccupation with nonessentials we waste ourselves and our hours. Give us, as well, a sense of unity, that we might find ways of common endeavor. So may Jesus Christ, in whose name we pray, be praised by us and our work. Amen.

GOD, OUR FATHER, you are the author of our life and the source of our every good. We believe in you and in your Son, Jesus Christ, and we acknowledge your leadership in all our affairs.

Come now, we pray, to this meeting. Give us direction and counsel. Help us learn about you and your work throughout the world.

Teach us, as well, to know one another better, that our brotherhood may extend beyond this time and these walls to encompass all of our life together.

Be with those who are absent, and with all who need you greatly, and give us the courage to be true disciples of your Son, our Savior Jesus Christ, in whose name we pray. Amen.

A YOUTH MEETING

ETERNAL FATHER, sometimes it seems as if the world has no place for us. We are no longer children, and yet the responsibilities and privileges of adulthood are denied us.

But we believe that in your sight we are of infinite worth, and we believe that we live in fulfillment of your intention and design.

Help us to be patient where patience is a virtue, and outspoken where wrongs ought to be righted, and helpful where we can make a meaningful contribution to our community. Direct us through our meeting together, and give us peace; through Christ, our Lord. Amen.

LORD JESUS CHRIST, we believe that you are the one way of truth and life in this world, but so often we seek other ways. Forgive us for our faithlessness, and protect us when we are tempted to forget you.

Show us how we can serve you in our daily lives, and give us courage for those times when we will be ridiculed or attacked because of our commitment to you.

Now be with us as we meet together in your name, and guide us to the doing of your will. Amen.

A MEETING WITH AN EMPHASIS
UPON WORLD MISSIONS

FATHER, we believe that you sent your Son Jesus Christ to our world in the fulness of your love. Because he came and taught your truth, and gave his life, your kingdom can come.

We know that in him we can have peace, and all people everywhere can live free of oppression and can grow into their full potential.

Set us, therefore, to the spread of this gospel. Help us to reach to others in love, but with respect for their culture and history. Guard us against equating our nation's aspirations and our service of your kingdom. Teach us humility, patience, and tact.

Keep us ever aware of your purposes, that we might come to others with your truth knowing that we do not thereby glorify ourselves, but your Son, our Saviour, in whose name we pray. Amen.

AT THE CLOSE OF THE MEETING

WE THANK YOU, Father, for the guidance you have given to us through this time. Now, as we go from here, give us a sense of real concern, one for another, and if we have in any way offended another, let there be forgiveness and a resolution of differences.

Keep us in safety on our homeward way, and increase our determination to live for you in all of life.

Bless us and keep us, Lord. Cause your face to shine upon us and be gracious to us. Lift up your countenance upon us, and give us peace. Amen.

A CHRISTMAS BANQUET

ALMOST EVERYTHING is ready, Lord. The decorations are up, the food is on the table, and the people who have planned the program are finished with their work. And we are here, all of us friends, happy together because it is the season of Christmas.

Yet even as the world needed you, and for that need you were born, so we need you too. Come, Lord Jesus, and be our guest. Fill us with joy at the memory of your birth, and with compassion for any who suffer and are in want, and with peace, one with another and within your world. Come, Lord Jesus. Amen.

AN EASTER SUNDAY BREAKFAST

LORD JESUS CHRIST, you rose victorious from death and the grave, and now we celebrate your life in our world. You are risen. You are risen indeed!

Come with your power among us, and give us newness of life. As you blessed the food by the Sea of Galilee, bless our food this day, and nourish us by your presence.

Cause our fellowship one with another to bind us closer in your service. Send us from here ready to tell others that you are the risen Lord of all of life, and keep us forever in your love. Amen.

BEFORE A BIBLE STUDY

SPIRIT OF GOD, we come together to learn of your work with our world as recorded in scripture. Open our minds to the implications for our lives.

Help us see the Bible as evidence of your involvement in the affairs of men, but prevent us from trying to use the word to prove our own opinions. Enable us, rather, to learn your will from scripture and from one another, and then send us to the doing of your word in the rest of life; through Christ, our Lord. Amen.

A SEMINARIAN'S GRADUATION

O SPIRIT OF GOD, we thank you for your continuing concern for your people. We believe that you work within us that we might know of your love, and that we are your instruments in the building of your church.

We are especially grateful for your influence in the life of   (name)   . We know that he (she) has taken direction because of those who have cared about him (her) through these past years, professors, friends, and family, and as you have moved in and through them, you have been his (her) helper and guide.

Now use him (her) that still others may find meaning for their lives. Minister to this world through him (her). Open his (her) mind to the truth of the word today, and his (her) heart to the needs of your people, that he (she) may be faithful to his (her) calling; through Christ, our Lord. Amen.

FOR THE PASTOR

ETERNAL FATHER, we are grateful for the leadership of our pastor in this congregation, and we thank you for his (her) call to serve with us. Uphold and sustain him (her) in his (her) work with the assurance of your presence and direction.

Encourage him (her) when he (she) is impatient or depressed. Guide him (her) when he (she) doubts his (her) course and reassure him (her) when his (her) faith is weak.

Speak to him (her) through us, and show us how we can participate in the ministry of our congregation with him (her) and support him (her) with our time, our talents, our resources, and our affection; through Christ, our Lord. Amen.

BEFORE COMMUNION

DEAR FATHER, quiet my mind and help me to believe as I come to receive communion. You know how easily I can be distracted. Send your Spirit, and help me understand the fulness of your continuing love for your people, that the sacrament may give strength for my life in your service; through Christ, our Lord. Amen.

AFTER COMMUNION

FATHER, thank you for the evidence of your love in the sacrament of communion. Keep me faithful to you and to your purpose for my life, and willing to follow your Son, Jesus Christ, in whose name I pray. Amen.

III. PRAYERS FOR

LAY MINISTRY AMONG FRIENDS

AND FAMILY

*Perhaps the prayers that mark a family's
life together are seldom thought of in terms of
ministry, yet they too are ways in which we
reach to one another's needs. This section
includes many such prayers covering the
day-to-day experiences of ordinary life as
well as the special times when special events
are observed.*

*The possibilities of lay ministry to the sick
need to be emphasized. This is another area
in which we have depended upon the work of
the ordained clergy, and while pastors receive
special training for this phase of their profession,
and accomplish much good, they would welcome
the further ministry of devoted lay persons to
those who are ill or in adversity. A brief visit,
a few friendly words of encouragement, and a
short scripture reading and prayer could be a
way of showing concern and love. Probably
it would be helpful to talk with the pastor
before making a call.*

FOR FAMILY LIFE

WE THANK YOU, Father, for our families. We
celebrate the joy we have as we live through
the years together, our happy anniversaries,
our gift-giving and our special customs, our many
days of love. We think of you as the designer
of our family life, and we are grateful.

Keep us aware of our responsibilities to each
other. Save us from anger, and fault-finding,
and apathy. Move within us that we might
search out new ways of devotion, new
possibilities for service, new means of
commitment. Send your Spirit for our family's
good; through Jesus Christ, our Lord. Amen.

TABLE PRAYERS

YOU ARE the source of all good, Father. We
thank you for the gift of life, and for the things
we need for our lives. Be our guest at this meal,
and go with us throughout the rest of this day,
that we may live for you and for the service
of your people; through Christ, our Lord.
Amen.

FATHER GOD, we are grateful for all we have
from you: for our family and our loved ones,
for our useful occupations and the resources
that have been given to us, and now especially
for our food. Consecrate us to each other,
our lives to your service, and our meal to our
health and strength; through Christ, our Lord.
Amen.

YOU ARE THE SOURCE of all good in our lives,
O God, and the author of life itself. We thank you
for your goodness, for the bounty of the fields
and the work of those who have harvested and
prepared our food, and for the opportunities we
have to enrich our lives because of our families
and our friends. Make this meal a blessing, Father,
and us a blessing to others; through Christ, our
Lord. Amen.

ETERNAL FATHER, you give more than we
need or deserve, and we see evidence of your love
in all of life. We thank you now for our food,
and pray for strength that we may be enabled
to fulfill our responsibilities and serve your
kingdom; through Christ, our Lord. Amen.

MEALTIME PRAYERS FOR CHILDREN

DEAR JESUS, come and be our guest at this meal. Give us nourishment from our food, and help us to love one another more. Amen.

OUR FATHER, we thank you for our life, and for our home, for our friends and family, and for our food. Strengthen us so that we might do your will; through Jesus Christ, our Lord. Amen.

YOU HAVE GIVEN us all we have, dear Father, and now we are about to share this food that comes from you. Thank you for your love and kindness, and help us to show our gratitude by our service to other people; through Christ, our Lord. Amen.

DEAR FATHER, we thank you for all who have worked so that we might eat: the farmers, the processors, the storekeepers; and we thank you for those who earned the money to buy the food. Make us grateful to them all, and help us to help others; through Christ, our Lord. Amen.

WE THANK YOU, Father, for caring about us and reaching to us to meet our needs. Especially, now, are we grateful for the food set before us. Grant that it might strengthen our bodies to do your will; in the name of Jesus. Amen.

A WEDDING RECEPTION

FATHER, we honor the wedding of   (name)
and   (name)   . We take delight in their
union, and pray for their happiness through all
of their life together. Be with us in this time
of celebration, and consecrate our laughter and
our joy that we might be a blessing, one to
another, as a sign of the blessing of this
marriage; through Christ, our Lord. Amen.

A WEDDING ANNIVERSARY

FATHER, you have richly blessed our coming together as man and wife, and we rejoice in our union. Even when our circumstances have seemed difficult, you have enabled us by your power and your love.

Help us throughout all the days of our life together to turn to you, in sadness and in joy. So may we know you as the source of our good, even as we look to one another in continuing love and devotion, and serve one another as if we were serving you; through Christ, our Lord. Amen.

LORD JESUS CHRIST, as you blessed the wedding at Cana, you have blessed this marriage. As you transformed ordinary water into the best of wine, you have transformed the ordinary elements of life for   (name)   and
     (name)   into years of happiness.

We thank you for your love evident in their love. Continue to favor them with your presence, that through their life together in the future as in the past they will bear witness to their faith in you by their devotion to each other. Amen.

A TWENTY-FIFTH WEDDING ANNIVERSARY

FATHER, for twenty-five years you have watched over the marriage of   (name) and   (name)   .

You have been with them as their children have been born, and have grown and matured. You have gone with them as they have moved from one home to another. You have cared when they have suffered adversity, or illness, and when they have grieved because of a death in the family. You have been their companion as they have talked about the possibilities of new jobs and decorated living rooms and celebrated birthdays and thanksgivings and anniversaries and Christmasses.

Through all of their life together you have been together with them, and we are confident of your continuing presence through all of their future. We thank you for your love alive in their lives.

Give them, now, a deeper love for you and for each other, and new joy in their unity, and your peace; through Christ, our Lord. Amen.

A GOLDEN WEDDING ANNIVERSARY

HOW SWIFT the passage of the years, Father, and yet how full those years with grace and love by your will.

We thank you for the half century   (name) and   (name)   have lived together as man and wife. We thank you for their testimony to the enduring qualities of affection and fidelity and devotion. We thank you for all who have been touched by their lives and enriched by them.

Continue, we pray, to be their eternal God and Father. Give them joy for mourning, strength for weakness, the vision of the mountains for their times in the valley.

Surround us all with your love, that in our observance of this anniversary we may have an uplifting of our spirits and a deepening of our concerns one for another; through Christ, our Lord. Amen.

A CHILD'S BIRTHDAY

TODAY IS   (name)   's birthday, Father, and
we are very happy.

We thank you for giving us   (name)   ,
and we thank you for the love we have for one
another. Help   (name)   , so that today and
every day in his (her) life he (she) may have the
joy that comes only from you; through Christ,
our Lord. Amen.

AN ADULT'S BIRTHDAY

WE PRAISE YOU for this day, Lord Jesus
Christ, and for the birth we now celebrate. We
are grateful for that life, and for the bonds of
love and devotion that we share, one with
another.

Cause each new day of that life to shine
with useful service. By your sustaining power
continue to come and live in that life, that
there may continue to be meaning and peace.

Strengthen the regard and affection we hold
for each other. Let this day for the observing
of this birth be happy, and let all days that are
lived in your light be happy, even as long ago
men beheld your birth and your life, and
rejoiced. Amen.

BEFORE AN EXAMINATION

ETERNAL GOD, source of all truth, be with
(name)   as he (she) takes an examination in
(subject)   . Calm his (her) nervousness, clear
his (her) mind, and help him (her) to truly reveal
his (her) understanding of the subject.

Give him (her) perspective as well, with the
realization that wisdom begins with faith in
you; through Christ, our Lord. Amen.

BEFORE A JOB INTERVIEW

FATHER,   (name)   is about to be
interviewed for a position as a   (position)
with   (company)   . We do not know if this
work best suits his (her) interests and abilities,
but we believe that you can give the insight
necessary for a proper decision.

Accordingly, help him (her) at this time.
Keep him (her) alert and sensitive, so that
he (she) might create a good impression as well
as that he (she) might intelligently discern the
nature of this position, with its advantages and
disadvantages. Help   (name)   to follow
your will for his (her) life; through Christ, our
Lord. Amen.

THANKSGIVING DINNER

DEAR FATHER, you have given us our very
life and more than we can use of the treasures
of your world. Now we are gathered together
for this meal of thanksgiving, and we are once
again reminded of our blessings. We have this
abundance, and we have each other. We thank
you for your love.

Yet even as we feast, Father, many of your
children are in want, and are troubled. Look to
them in their needs, and challenge us to reach to
them with help, that our thankfulness might take
form in service, our faith in sacrifice; through
Jesus Christ, our Lord. Amen.

BEFORE GIFT-GIVING AT CHRISTMAS

LORD JESUS, because wise men came from far
away to see you and present their gifts, we
remember you by our gifts to each other. These
things we give are tokens of our love. But help
us to understand that it is when we give ourselves
that we give the best of gifts. Even as you came
to give yourself for the world, let us seek new
ways of service to you and to each other and to
your world, so that there might be peace on
earth and good will toward men. Amen.

FOLLOWING CHILDBIRTH

AND THEY were bringing children to him, that he might touch them; and the disciples rebuked them. But when Jesus saw it he was indignant, and said to them, "Let the children come to me, do not hinder them; for to such belongs the kingdom of God. Truly, I say to you, whoever does not receive the kingdom of God like a child shall not enter it." And he took them in his arms and blessed them, laying his hands upon them.

Mark 10:13-16

LORD JESUS CHRIST, you blessed the children, and commended their example because of their innocence and trustfulness. We are thankful for the gift of a child to this family. Be with all who are united by this birth, the parents and their loved ones and their friends, and be with the child whose life has now begun. Grant that by growing together in faith and concern, one for another, they may give evidence of the presence on this earth of your kingdom. Amen.

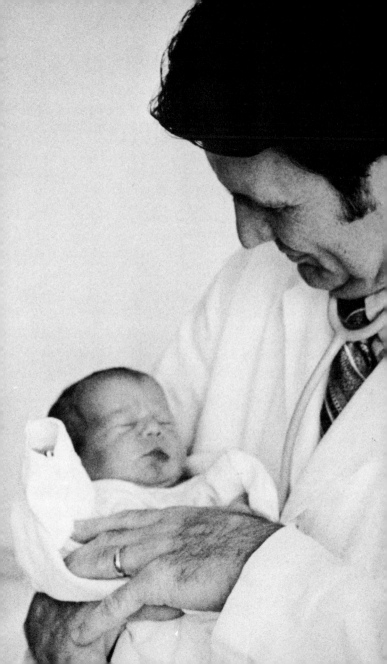

AT THE BAPTISM OF A CHILD

ETERNAL FATHER, you have received this child by baptism into your church, and we thank you for this further sign of your concern for your people.

Continue to be with   (child's name)   and his (her) parents. Help them to live in love one to another, and to serve one another with devotion. As you have given promise of forgiveness and peace, may they live in that grace, and close to your Son, Jesus, in whose name we pray. Amen.

AT CONFIRMATION

LORD JESUS CHRIST, you call us to be your disciples on earth, and we thank you for that opportunity. Help us to serve you by the way we live our lives in loving service of your people.

We are especially grateful for your guidance given to   (name)   , who now has confirmed his (her) belief in you and promised to be faithful. Keep him (her) strong in that conviction, able to withstand the pressures of this world with its temptations, and alert to your will, that he (she) may belong to your kingdom forever. Amen.

FOR ONE WHO IS SICK

AND PETER answered him, "Lord, if it is you,
bid me come to you on the water." He said,
"Come." So Peter got out of the boat and
walked on the water and came to Jesus: but when
he saw the wind, he was afraid, and beginning
to sink he cried out, "Lord, save me." Jesus
immediately reached out his hand and caught
him, saying to him, "O man of little faith, why
did you doubt?" And when they got into the
boat, the wind ceased. And those in the boat
worshipped him, saying, "Truly you are the Son
of God."

Matthew 14:28-33

JESUS, we can do anything by your power, but
we grow fearful and we fail. Even then you can
save us. Be with your servant   (name)   .
Give him (her) new ability to believe in you and
trust your power. Work through those who
minister to   (name)   , his (her) loved ones,
friends, and doctor, and be as a great physician
to him (her), that by your will there may be new
strength and health and the trust that comes from
believing in you. Amen.

REJOICE in the Lord always; again I will say,
Rejoice. Let all men know your forbearance.
The Lord is at hand. Have no anxiety about
anything, but in everything by prayer and
supplication with thanksgiving let your requests
be made known to God. And the peace of God,
which passes all understanding, will keep your
hearts and your minds in Christ Jesus.

Philippians 4:4-7

WE DO REJOICE in you, Lord Jesus, for we
know that you are at hand, and we need have
no anxiety about anything. By the instruction
of your word we are to let our requests be made
known by prayer and supplication with
thanksgiving. Accordingly we pray for this
your servant, that he (she) may be given new
strength, and healing, and above all else that
peace which passes understanding through your
love. Amen.

FOR ONE WHO IS SICK IN A HOSPITAL

SO WE DO NOT lose heart. Though our outer
nature is wasting away, our inner nature is being
renewed every day. For this slight momentary
affliction is preparing for us an eternal weight of
glory beyond all comparison, because we look
not to the things that are seen but to the things
that are unseen; for the things that are seen are
transient, but the things that are unseen are
eternal.

2 Corinthians 4:16-18

FATHER, we are confident that our infirmities
are only slight momentary afflictions preparing
us for a life with you that will be beyond all
comparison. We do not lose heart.

Yet we are weak, and sometimes our faith
seems severely tested. When that happens,
remind us of your loving power, and restore
our understanding of your continuing concern
for us.

Look now to this your servant. By your
mercy and will help him (her) to come to new
strength and health. Work through those who
serve him (her) here, the doctors and nurses
and others, and help him (her) to look to those
things that are unseen, but in your hands;
through Christ, our Lord. Amen.

THEREFORE, since we are justified by faith, we have peace with God through our Lord Jesus Christ. Through him we have obtained access to this grace in which we stand, and we rejoice in our hope of sharing the glory of God. More than that, we rejoice in our sufferings, knowing that suffering produces endurance, and endurance produces character, and character produces hope, and hope does not disappoint us, because God's love has been poured into our hearts through the Holy Spirit which has been given to us.

Romans 5:1-5

FATHER, by your instruction we ought to rejoice in our sufferings, because suffering produces endurance, and endurance character, and character hope. But you know our fears and our weaknesses. You know how difficult it is for us to have hope. We need the assurance of your love.

Come with your Spirit to this room. Help those who seek to be of help in this place, the doctors and nurses and orderlies, the members of   (name)   's family and his (her) friends. By your will give relief from pain and a new measure of health, and all things needful for his (her) life; through Christ, our Lord. Amen.

WHEN HE came down from the mountain, great
crowds followed him; and behold, a leper came to
him and knelt before him, saying, "Lord, if you
will, you can make me clean." And he stretched
out his hand and touched him, saying, "I will; be
clean."

Matthew 8:1-3

JESUS, it is by your will that we regain our
strength and health, even as it is not your will
that we suffer. We ask that your will be done
for   (name)   .

Work through those who serve him (her) here,
his (her) doctors and nurses and all others.
Give them insight and understanding; sharpen
their skills and deepen their compassion.

Grant, as well, that   (name)   may so trust
in you and in your love that anxieties flee, and
apprehensions dissolve. By the care of devoted
men and women, and by an inner peace, and by
the assurance of your continuing presence, cause
healing to come. Amen.

> "ASK, and it will be given you; seek and you will find; knock, and it will be opened to you. For every one who asks receives, and he who seeks finds, and to him who knocks it will be opened."
>
> *Matthew 7:7-8*

O LORD JESUS, you have promised that if we ask we shall receive; that if we search we shall find; that if we but knock upon the door that bars us from your love, it will be opened.

We ask, by your instruction, for the health of   (name)   . We search for an understanding of the adversities of life. We pause before the fulness of your concern for us, knowing that you are enough for all our needs.

Come now with your power. Guide all who minister here, doctors, nurses, technicians, and others. Surround   (name)   with your presence, and give your peace. Amen.

BEFORE AN OPERATION

AND WHEN he got into the boat, his disciples
followed him. And behold, there arose a great
storm on the sea, so that the boat was being swamped
by the waves; but he was asleep. And they went and
woke him, saying, "Save, Lord; we are perishing." And
he said to them, "Why are you afraid, O men of little
faith?" Then he rose and rebuked the winds and the
sea; and there was a great calm. And the men
marveled, saying, "What sort of man is this, that
even winds and sea obey him?" *Matthew 8:23-27*

LORD JESUS, sometimes we are almost swamped
by the circumstances of our lives. Yet we know
that you have the power to still the storms and make
all things well again.

Come with your power to   (name)   . Guide
the hands of those who will shortly be responsible
for surgery. Grant that he (she) may enter upon
that time with confidence in your love, and as it
may be your will, give a quick return to strength
and health. Amen.

IMMEDIATELY AFTER SURGERY

FATHER, reach with your love to   (name)
Give patience under adversity, relief from pain
and discomfort, and the sure knowledge of your
presence. So may he (she) have a healing rest,
and your peace; through Christ, our Lord. Amen.

A TERMINAL ILLNESS

FOR GOD so loved the world that he gave his only Son, that whoever believes in him should not perish but have eternal life. For God sent the Son into the world, not to condemn the world, but that the world might be saved through him.
John 3:16-17

O GOD, we see your love in the gift of your Son, Jesus. Through him we know of your will for your people, in that we are to live, and not die. Help us to have new faith in your promises, so that we need not fear for ourselves or for the ones we love.

Be with   (name)   . Give relief from pain and discomfort, the assurance of your presence, and confidence in your love; through Christ, our Lord. Amen.

"I AM the good shepherd; I know my own and my own know me, as the Father knows me and I know the Father; and I lay down my life for the sheep." *John 10:14-15*

LORD JESUS CHRIST, you are the good shepherd, and you give your life for us. When adversity causes us to become discouraged, we can trust you. When pain and darkness close in on us, you are with us. We believe in you. Help us when we cannot believe, and restore us, for we know that all things work together for good to those who love you. Amen.

BEREAVEMENT

"LET NOT your hearts be troubled; believe in God, believe also in me. In my Father's house are many rooms; if it were not so, would I have told you that I go to prepare a place for you? And when I go and prepare a place for you, I will come again and will take you to myself, that where I am you may be also. And you know the way where I am going." Thomas said to him, "Lord, we do not know where you are going; how can we know the way?" Jesus said to him, "I am the way, and the truth, and the life; no one comes to the Father, but by me."

John 14:1-6

JESUS, we believe that you are the way, the truth, and the life, and we know that in your Father's house are many rooms.

We thank you for the life that has been lived, now with you forever. We thank you for every evidence of your grace which has been known through that life, for love and devotion, for concern and joy.

Be with those who mourn. Give them fresh assurance of your love, and strength for these days of trial, and comfort for their grief. Amen.

THEN I SAW a new heaven and a new earth; for the first heaven and the first earth had passed away, and the sea was no more. And I saw the holy city, new Jerusalem, coming down out of heaven from God, prepared as a bride adorned for her husband; and I heard a loud voice from the throne saying, "Behold, the dwelling of God is with men. He will dwell with them, and they shall be his people, and God himself will be with them; he will wipe away every tear from their eyes, and death shall be no more, neither shall there be mourning nor crying nor pain any more, for the former things have passed away."

Revelation 21:1-4

FATHER, we know that we will dwell with you in a life without tears and death. But now our vision is unclear, and we are overcome by sorrow and despair.

Strengthen our faith. Reassure us of your love. Remove our doubts and our regrets by the sure and certain awareness that the end of life on this earth is the beginning of our life forever with you.

Uphold this family in this time of stress, help them to grow closer to each other and to you, and give them your peace; through Christ, our Lord. Amen.

IN THE MORNING

A NEW DAY is upon us, Lord, and we rejoice in its promise and opportunity. We thank you for the gift of life, and for bringing us to this time. We thank you for all the good things we share, for friends and families, for useful occupations and pleasant diversions, and for your continuing love.

Now go with us through this day. Give us patience for its unfinished labors, perspective for its disappointments, and humility for its victories, for we believe that all we are and have is by your grace. Turn us away from evil, and into paths of service to others; through Jesus Christ, our Saviour. Amen.

A CHILD'S EVENING PRAYERS

DEAR FATHER, the night has come and this day is over. Thank you for the good things that have happened. Thank you for my friends and my family. Thank you for my school and my teachers, for my church and its pastor, and for all the people whose work helps to make the world a better place.

Some need you greatly, and I pray for them. If they are unhappy or sick or poor, come to them with whatever is most needed.

Be with me through this night, and go with me through tomorrow, so that my life might reflect your will; through Christ, our Lord. Amen.

DEAR FATHER, thank you for this day, for friends and family, for school and church, and for all you have given to me, even for life itself.

Now help me to have a peaceful rest so that I might be strengthened for tomorrow; through Jesus Christ, your Son, our Lord. Amen.

FATHER, you are greater than all of the universe, and yet you know about me, and you care for me. Thank you for your love, and thank you for my life, and thank you for my family and friends. Keep them safe, and give them all their needs.

Help me with my school work, and with all of my life, so that I might better follow the example of your Son Jesus, in whose name I pray. Amen.

LORD JESUS CHRIST, you were once a youth, and you increased in wisdom and in stature as you grew older. Help me as I grow older. Guide me with my studies. Show me how to be patient and kind with other people. Encourage me to make the right decisions about my life and conduct. Be with me through this night, so that I might sleep well and gain new strength for tomorrow, better to serve you and your people. Amen.

AN ADULT'S EVENING PRAYERS

FATHER, you know me and my life. You see through my pretensions and my excuses. You know the depth of my frustrations as well as the sincerity of my desires to be of worth to myself and to others.

Now my day has come to its close, and its events are once more passing through my mind, and the troubles of tomorrow loom large before me. Come with your peace to my life. Ease the anguish and the misgiving and the bitterness. Grant me the grace to let this day go to the unchangeable past and the courage to greet the future without worry, because you are with me; through Christ, our Lord. Amen.

NOW IS THE TIME of shadows and rest, dear Lord. Now is the time when silence finally descends upon this home and the people within these walls. Now is the time to gather together the hundreds of different threads of this day, and think them through, and ask for your help.

I am confident about you. I am sure of your love. In that trust I ask you, now, to reach with your care and your strength to these special needs:

    [someone who is ill, or troubled, or otherwise
      in difficulty]
    [a disappointment, a failure, or a setback]
    [an enemy's problems]

[the concerns of loved ones]
[a grave situation in the nation or in the world]
[other personal needs]
Now give me a quiet rest, and new strength
for the tasks of the morning; through Christ, our
Lord. Amen.

DEAR FATHER, this has been a good day in my
life, and I thank and praise you for all that has
happened because of which I can be joyful.
Especially do I thank you for:
[a vocational accomplishment]
[a personal accomplishment]
[the kindness of a friend]
[the love of another person]
[a great happiness]
Yet there are those whose hearts are heavy
with apprehension and sorrow, Father. Be with
them and give them new measures of faith and
hope. Look upon the sick and injured, those
who are the victims of oppression and injustice,
those who are lost and alone.
Help me to help others, and show me how to
live in greater imitation of your Son, Jesus
Christ, our Lord, in whose name I pray. Amen.

BEFORE A LOVED ONE'S JOURNEY

DEAR FATHER, (name) is about to leave for (place) . Because we care greatly about him (her), we ask your protection for the journey. Grant a safe passage, but if danger should occur, give him (her) whatever may be needed for the circumstance. Ease our anxieties over parting, and assure us of our bond across the miles because of our common faith in your love. Grant a reunion in good time, and until then give us the joy of happy memories and the fulness of your peace; through Christ, our Lord. Amen.

UPON BEGINNING A JOURNEY

FATHER, we ask for your protection and care as we leave for (destination) . Keep us alert and perceptive so that we might not be the cause of an accident, give us patience should we be delayed, and help us to be considerate of others who are also traveling. So may we have a pleasant and safe journey; through Christ, our Lord. Amen.

UPON PARTING

FATHER, we believe that you live in human affairs, and that even as you have brought us together, you will do so again. Be with us as we go our separate ways. Strengthen our concern for one another. Protect us from harm and danger, and keep us in your care; through Christ, our Lord. Amen.

THE LORD'S PRAYER

Our Father in heaven,
   holy be your Name,
   your kingdom come,
   your will be done,
      on earth as in heaven.
Give us today our daily bread.
Forgive us our sins
   as we forgive those who sin against us.
Do not bring us to the test
   but deliver us from evil.

For the kingdom, the power, and the glory are yours
   now and for ever.

*The above text is as adopted by the International
Consultation on English Texts, which includes
Lutheran, Episcopal, and Roman Catholic
representatives from the United States and Canada,
and Anglican, Roman Catholic, Methodist, Baptist,
Presbyterian, and Congregationalist members from
England, Ireland, Scotland, and Wales.*